Presidents

GEORGE
WASHINGTON

A MyReportLinks.com Book

Stephen Feinstein

MyReportLinks.com Books

an imprint of

Enslow Publishers, Inc.

Box 398, 40 Industrial Road
Berkeley Heights, NJ 07922
USA

MyReportLinks.com Books, an imprint of Enslow Publishers, Inc.

Copyright © 2002 by Enslow Publishers, Inc.

Library of Congress Cataloging-in-Publication Data

Feinstein, Stephen.
George Washington: a MyReportLinks.com book / Stephen Feinstein.
        p. cm. — (Presidents)
    Includes bibliographical references and (p.) index.
    Summary: Traces the life of America's first president, known as the "Father of
his Country."
    ISBN 0-7660-5000-9
    1. Washington, George, 1732–1799—Juvenile literature. 2. Presidents—
United States—Biography—Juvenile literature. [1. Washington, George,
1732–1799. 2. Presidents.] I. Title. II. Series.
    E312.66 .F45 2002
    973.4'1'092—dc21   2001004299

Printed in the United States of America

10 9 8 7 6 5 4 3 2 1

To Our Readers: We have done our best to make sure all Internet addresses in this book were active and appropriate when we went to press. However, the author and the Publisher have no control over, and assume no liability for, the material available on those Internet sites or on other Web sites they may link to. The Publisher will try to keep the Report Links that back up this book up to date on our Web site for three years from the book's first publication date. Any comments or suggestions can be sent by e-mail to comments@myreportlinks.com or to the address on the back cover.

Photo Credits: © Corel Corporation, pp. 1 (background), 3, 16; Courtesy of America's Library, p. 33; Courtesy of 1st Battalion, 14th Infantry Division Homepage, p. 30; Courtesy of George Washington Online, p. 11; Courtesy of MyReportLinks.com Books, p. 4; Courtesy of National Park Service, pp. 15, 21, 45; Courtesy of Public Broadcasting Service: "Chronicle of the Revolution," p. 26; *Dictionary of American Portraits*, © 1967 Dover Publications, Inc., pp. 40, 43; Library of Congress, pp. 1, 18, 22, 28, 34, 37; National Archives, pp. 32, 36; The Library of Virginia, p. 13.

Cover Photo: © Corel Corporation, Library of Congress.

Contents

About MyReportLinks.com Books

MyReportLinks.com Books
Great Books, Great Links, Great for Research!

MyReportLinks.com Books present the information you need to learn about your report subject. In addition, they show you where to go on the Internet for more information. The pre-evaluated Report Links, listed on **www.myreportlinks.com**, save hours of research time and link to dozens—even hundreds—of Web sites, source documents, and photos related to your report topic.

To Our Readers:

Each Report Link has been reviewed by our editors, who will work hard to keep only active and appropriate Internet addresses in our books and up to date on our Web site. However, the author and the Publisher have no control over, and assume no liability for, the material available on those Internet sites, or on other Web sites they may link to.

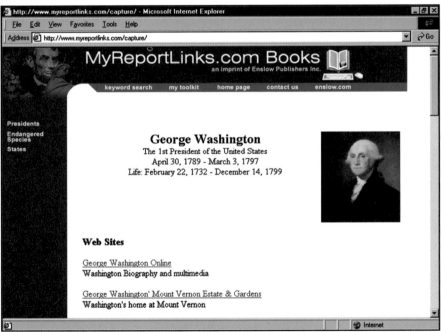

Access:

The Publisher will try to keep the Report Links that back up this book up to date on our Web site for three years from the book's first publication date. Please enter **PWA1283** if asked for a password.

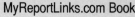

MyReportLinks.com Books

Tools　　Search　　Notes　　Discuss　　　　　　　　　　Go!

Report Links

> The Internet sites described below can be accessed at
> **http://www.myreportlinks.com**

EDITOR'S CHOICE

George Washington Online
George Washington Online offers a complete look at the life of America's first president. From the writings of this great man, to modern essays on his character, Washington is analyzed completely. Multimedia presentations of his essays are also available.

Link to this Internet site from http://www.myreportlinks.com

EDITOR'S CHOICE

The American Presidency
At this site you will find objects related to all the presidents of the United States, including George Washington. You can also read a brief description of the era he lived in and learn about the office of the presidency.

Link to this Internet site from http://www.myreportlinks.com

EDITOR'S CHOICE

Explore the Amazing World of Early America
This collection of documents and essays paints a colorful portrait of colonial America. Included in the collection are such famous documents as the United States Constitution, Declaration of Independence, and Bill of Rights.

Link to this Internet site from http://www.myreportlinks.com

EDITOR'S CHOICE

America's Story: Martha Washington Died
The Library of Congress presents "America's Story," a site created specifically for young adults, and dedicated to the history of the United States. Here a brief biography of Martha Washington is presented.

Link to this Internet site from http://www.myreportlinks.com

EDITOR'S CHOICE

George Washington Papers at the Library of Congress, 1741–1799
With more than sixty thousand documents, the Library of Congress holds the largest collection of Washington's papers in the world. Browse through Washington's diaries, correspondence, and speeches.

Link to this Internet site from http://www.myreportlinks.com

EDITOR'S CHOICE

American History Documents
Indiana University's Lilly Library presents a collection of historical documents from early America. Of these primary sources, two are in Washington's own handwriting.

Link to this Internet site from http://www.myreportlinks.com

The Internet sites described below can be accessed at
http://www.myreportlinks.com

The American President: George Washington, 1st President of the United States

The American President site offers a good introduction to Washington's life by providing quick facts as well as a detailed biography.

Link to this Internet site from http://www.myreportlinks.com

The American Revolution and Its Era

This collection of maps and charts from the Library of Congress brings to life the Revolutionary War and the period leading up to it. The maps reveal a country much different than the one we know today.

Link to this Internet site from http://www.myreportlinks.com

The First Ladies of the United States: Martha Dandridge Custis Washington

This site offers a brief biography of Martha Washington, a look at her contributions in shaping Washington's legacy, and the role of future first ladies.

Link to this Internet site from http://www.myreportlinks.com

G. Washington: Biography

This clearly written biography is a good place to begin research on Washington. The profile is divided into seven sections, covering Washington's early life through his retirement.

Link to this Internet site from http://www.myreportlinks.com

George Washington's Birthplace

In 1732, Washington was born at Pope's Creek Plantation. The home had been in his family's hands since 1658. Americans began touring this historic spot as early as 1815. This site, maintained by the National Park Service, provides a history of Washington's birthplace.

Link to this Internet site from http://www.myreportlinks.com

George Washington: Farewell Address, Philadelphia, PA, 1796-09-17

On September 17, 1796, George Washington published his farewell speech to the nation. This site contains the full text of the farewell address as well as photographs of stamps and currency with Washington's likeness.

Link to this Internet site from http://www.myreportlinks.com

The Internet sites described below can be accessed at
http://www.myreportlinks.com

▶ George Washington, Mapmaker

When Washington was only sixteen, he helped survey the properties of
Lord Fairfax in Virginia's Shenandoah Valley. The Library of Congress
site offers a brief history of Washington's time as a surveyor, as well as
maps he either created or annotated.

Link to this Internet site from http://www.myreportlinks.com

▶ George Washington Memorial Parkway

The George Washington Memorial parkway runs through the Virginia
countryside. Many historical places lie along the parkway, including
Mount Vernon. This National Park Service site tells the story of the
Parkway and the places that it connects.

Link to this Internet site from http://www.myreportlinks.com

▶ George Washington Quiz

Even before Washington's death in 1799, villages such as Old
Sturbridge Village would celebrate his birthday with a festival. This
Web site provides a great quiz that tests student's knowledge of the fact
and fiction of America's first president.

Link to this Internet site from http://www.myreportlinks.com

▶ George and Martha Washington: Portraits from the Presidential Years

This site was created in conjunction with a 1999 exhibition of
Washington portraits at the National Portrait Gallery. On display are
some of the most famous paintings of the Washingtons.

Link to this Internet site from http://www.myreportlinks.com

▶ Historic Valley Forge

From late 1777 until the late spring of 1778 the Continental Army of
the United States camped out at Valley Forge, Pennsylvania. This site
tells the story of that famous encampment and much more about
Washington and his military service.

Link to this Internet site from http://www.myreportlinks.com

▶ "I Do Solemnly Swear . . ."

This collection contains a wealth of documents and images related to
presidential inaugurations. Both of Washington's inaugural addresses
are presented, as well as portraits and video presentations for a few
presidents.

Link to this Internet site from http://www.myreportlinks.com

Report Links

The Internet sites described below can be accessed at
http://www.myreportlinks.com

LIBERTY! The American Revolution
This site is a companion to the PBS series on the American Revolution. It discusses how the colonies gained independence from Britain and what liberty and freedom means today. Included is an index of related topics, objects used by colonial America, and a game that explores the events of the war.

Link to this Internet site from http://www.myreportlinks.com

The Life of George Washington
Historian David Ramsay published his biography of George Washington in 1807, eight years after Washington's death. This site features the full text of Ramsay's biography, along with photos of the original book and its title page.

Link to this Internet site from http://www.myreportlinks.com

The Life of George Washington
In 1999, Anne Petri, wife of U.S. Representative Tom Petri of Wisconsin, wrote a collection of essays about Washington to mark the bicentennial of his death. Among the subjects covered in Anne Petri's essays are Washington's involvement in architecture and farming.

Link to this Internet site from http://www.myreportlinks.com

Mary Washington House
The Association for the Preservation of Virginia Antiques cares for the historical locations in Virginia. One such spot is the home of Mary Ball Washington, George Washington's mother. This site provides a description of her home, the important political guests who visited, and a link to her biography.

Link to this Internet site from http://www.myreportlinks.com

Montcalm and Wolfe: The French and Indian War
The French and Indian War began in 1754. At the time, George Washington was a major in the British army. This site explores the war, which was a key event in the history of British rule in North America.

Link to this Internet site from http://www.myreportlinks.com

National Archives and Records Administration: American Originals
When Washington delivered his first inaugural address in 1789, he faced the challenge of leading a young country under a new and untried system of government. This site contains the full text of that address and photos of two of the original pages.

Link to this Internet site from http://www.myreportlinks.com

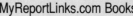
Report Links

The Internet sites described below can be accessed at http://www.myreportlinks.com

The Papers of George Washington
In 1969, the University of Virginia and Mount Vernon Ladies' Association of the Union began a project to assemble a complete collection of Washington's correspondence. Documents already available online chronicle his years in public service.

Link to this Internet site from http://www.myreportlinks.com

Sulgrave Manor: Home of George Washington's Ancestors
Like most Americans, George Washington could trace his roots to somewhere outside of the United States. This site offers a brief history of the Washington family, and information about its ancestral home at Sulgrave Manor, about 70 miles from London.

Link to this Internet site from http://www.myreportlinks.com

Ten Crucial Days
Washington's crossing of the Delaware River, is described by George Athan Billias on the 14th Battalion of the United States Army Web site. The site also describes some myths about the famous painting of the crossing.

Link to this Internet site from http://www.myreportlinks.com

The Washington Monument: Tribute in Stone
This National Park Service site is part of their "Teaching with Historic Places" program. The site focuses on the plans for Washington, D.C., and the history of the Washington Monument. It offers great images and facts for students, as well as lesson plans and ideas for teachers.

Link to this Internet site from http://www.myreportlinks.com

The White House: George Washington
This biography is part of the presidential profiles maintained by the official White House Web site. It offers an introductory overview of Washington's life, achievements and political philosophy.

Link to this Internet site from http://www.myreportlinks.com

The Winning of Independence, 1777–1783
This site traces America's struggle for independence, from Britain's early attempt to crush the revolting colonies, to the eventual victory of American forces. The text provides an excellent overview of the American Revolution.

Link to this Internet site from http://www.myreportlinks.com

Highlights

1732—*Feb. 22:* Washington is born in Westmoreland County, Virginia.

1753—Delivers message from Governor Dinwiddie to the French, demanding that the French withdraw from British territory.

1754–1758—Commands troops in battles during the French and Indian War.

1758—*Dec.:* Resigns from militia to begin serving in Virginia House of Burgesses.

1759—*Jan. 6:* Marries Martha Dandridge Custis.

1774—Elected delegate to First Continental Congress.

1775—Elected delegate to Second Continental Congress.

1775—*June 15:* Elected commander in chief of Continental Army.

1776—*Dec.:* Washington leads Continental Army to victory at the Battle of Trenton.

1781—*Oct. 19:* Defeats General Cornwallis at Yorktown forcing the British to surrender.

1787—*May 25:* Elected president of the Constitutional Convention.

1789—Elected first president of the United States.

April 30: Gives first inaugural address.

1792—Reelected president of the United States.

1793—*March 4:* Gives second inaugural address.

1796—*Sep. 19:* Washington's Farewell Address is printed in *American Daily Advertiser*, a Philadelphia newspaper. In it, he refuses a third term in office.

1798—*July 4:* Commissioned lieutenant general and commander in chief of the new U.S. Army.

1799—*Dec. 14:* Dies at Mount Vernon, Virginia.

Chapter 1 ▶

A Bold Gamble, December 25, 1776

The clouds were thickening above the Delaware River on December 25, 1776. It grew colder as the day wore on. Around two o'clock in the afternoon, General George Washington, commander of the Continental Army, marched his men to the Pennsylvania shore of the river. The twenty-four hundred American troops were cold and

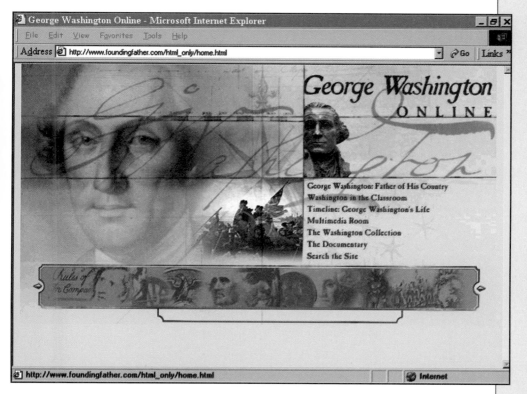

▲ As the leader of the Continental Army, it was up to George Washington to inspire his troops to win the war against Great Britain.

hungry. Some were without shoes. Their bruised feet left a bloody trail on the snow-covered ground.

At the outbreak of the American Revolution earlier that year, Washington's army had driven the British out of Boston. Since then the Patriots had suffered one defeat after another at the hands of the British. Indeed, the British commanders no longer regarded the Continental Army as a serious fighting force, and they expected that the Americans would soon give up the struggle. In a bold gamble born of desperation, Washington decided to carry out a surprise attack on the British outpost at Trenton, New Jersey. If the attack did not succeed, it would be the end of the Continental Army. The American Revolution would end in failure, then and there.

▶ Boosting Morale

Before ordering his soldiers into the barges that would ferry them across the river from Pennsylvania to New Jersey, Washington tried to raise their spirits. He handed his officers copies of an essay written just days before by the patriotic journalist Thomas Paine. The officers read these words to the men:

> These are the times that try men's souls. The summer soldier and the sunshine patriot will, in this crisis, shrink from the service of their country; but he that stands it now, deserves the love and thanks of man and woman. Tyranny, like hell, is not easily conquered; yet we have this consolation with us, that the harder the conflict, the more glorious the triumph.[1]

Thomas Paine's stirring words filled the soldiers with fresh energy and determination. The first flotilla of barges, loaded with men, horses, and artillery, set off across the ice-choked river. Washington went with them. The wind had picked up and it became difficult to see as snow and sleet whipped into the men's faces. The soldiers rowing the boats struggled to make headway as the oars caught against the floating chunks of ice. When they finally reached the opposite shore, Washington remained with the troops. The boats went back for the rest of the army.

The storm intensified as darkness descended on the troops huddled along the banks of the New Jersey side of the Delaware. The barges were still struggling back and forth across the river. As Washington watched their slow progress, he grew impatient. He had planned to launch a

Washington's victory at Trenton became a turning point in the Revolutionary War. It renewed America's hope for freedom.

surprise attack before dawn, under cover of darkness. Now it seemed less and less likely that this would be possible. The final contingent of troops did not reach the New Jersey side of the river until 4:00 A.M. Washington immediately ordered the men to begin marching. It was bitter cold, still snowing, and Trenton was ten miles away.

▶ Surprise Attack

The British outpost at Trenton was manned by German troops, known as Hessians. The Hessians were mercenary troops; professional soldiers who had been hired by the British to help them fight the Americans. Just as Washington had hoped, the Hessians had spent Christmas Day feasting and drinking. When Washington's army reached Trenton at eight o'clock, the Hessians were sound asleep. Once the attack began, they were unable to rouse themselves in time to organize a defense. Washington led his troops to a total victory, killing thirty Hessians and taking nine hundred prisoners.

By winning the day in Trenton, Washington not only saved his army, but also probably saved the American Revolution itself.[2] Twelve years later, a grateful new American nation would choose George Washington to become its first president.

Early Years, 1732–1759

George Washington, the man who is known as the "father of his country," was born in the colony of Virginia on February 22, 1732. He was Augustine and Mary Ball Washington's first child. When he was born, the Washingtons were living in a brick farmhouse on a plantation along the banks of the Potomac River. The plantation was known as Pope's Creek.

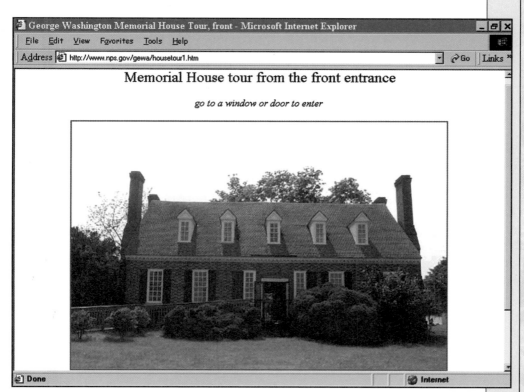

George Washington Memorial House Tour, front - Microsoft Internet Explorer

File   Edit   View   Favorites   Tools   Help

Address http://www.nps.gov/gewa/housetour1.htm   Go   Links

Memorial House tour from the front entrance

go to a window or door to enter

Done   Internet

▲ Washington was born on his parent's plantation, Pope's Creek. In 1932, this memorial house was erected. It was built to be very similar to Washington's birthplace.

▶ Childhood

When George was three, his family moved to a larger farmhouse forty miles away from Pope's Creek. The new house, which sat on a bluff above the Potomac, was eventually named Mount Vernon. In December 1738, when George was six, the restless Augustine once again moved the family to another of his properties, this time to Ferry Farm on the Rappahannock River.

Ferry Farm was a lively place. A ferry ran back and forth across the river from the Washington property to the town of Fredericksburg. Travelers would often spend the night at Ferry Farm, and George never lacked for company. He had three younger brothers and a younger sister as playmates. He also had two older half brothers. He was

▲ George first moved to Mount Vernon as a boy. He spent many happy years on this plantation, and in turn lived there throughout his adult life.

especially fond of Lawrence, who was fourteen years older than himself. Lawrence and George's other half brother, Augustine, had been educated in England. Lawrence had then become a British military officer. George admired his brother and his bright red uniform. He hoped that he also could one day join the British Army.

George expected that he, too, would be sent to England for his education. But in 1743, when he was eleven, his father died of a sudden illness. Lawrence inherited the Mount Vernon property and moved there. Augustine inherited Pope's Creek and went to live there. There was no money to send George to school in England. As a result, his education did not go very far beyond his boyhood studies of mathematics, English literature, Latin, and astronomy.

George's future seemed somewhat uncertain. The family disagreed on which direction his life should take. At fourteen, he was no longer a child, but a tall young man filled with energy. He was ready to make his way in the world. Lawrence arranged for George to become a midshipman on a vessel in the British Navy. George's mother did not allow this, so instead he eventually moved to Lawrence's home at Mount Vernon.

Learning a Trade

At Mount Vernon, George became a skilled horseman and learned to shoot well. He also became interested in surveying land, which involves measuring, and sketching maps. He had inherited his father's surveying instruments, and he learned something about the trade from local surveyors.

Lawrence was married to Anne Fairfax, and George was treated as a member of the family at the neighboring Fairfax plantation, called Belvoir. Anne's father, Colonel William

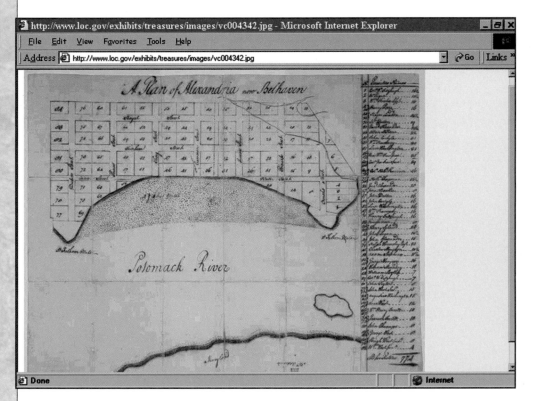

▲ *At age sixteen George Washington began a career in surveying. Throughout his life he enjoyed making maps of the wilderness and towns. This is his survey of Alexandria, Virginia, a town that borders Washington, D.C.*

Fairfax, was the cousin of Lord Fairfax, a powerful English nobleman. When Lord Fairfax came to visit, George took part in the Fairfax family's fox hunts. Lord Fairfax was impressed by young George's skills as a marksman and rider.

Lord Fairfax owned about five million acres of land in the wilderness of the Shenandoah Valley. In 1748, he set out with a party to survey his land holdings. Sixteen-year-old George was invited to join the group. The trip, which took about a month, was a grand adventure. George guided horses as they swam across a river, met a party of American

Indians, and learned enough about surveying to become a professional surveyor.

For the next three years, George surveyed wilderness territory throughout the Blue Ridge Mountains and other parts of northern Virginia. During this time, he acquired about fifteen hundred acres of his own land close by in the Shenandoah Valley.

In late 1751, George's brother Lawrence was stricken with tuberculosis. The two young men undertook a trip to Barbados in the West Indies, hoping the tropical climate would be good for Lawrence's health. While he was in Barbados, George became ill with smallpox. Luckily, he survived, but his face was forever scarred with pockmarks. Lawrence's condition only worsened. Upon their return six months later, Lawrence died from the tuberculosis.

Militiaman

George Washington, now twenty, sought to be appointed adjutant general of the Virginia militia, a post vacated by the death of Lawrence. He made social calls on various members of the Virginia government. Amazingly, he was given the rank of major, even though he had never had any military training.

The following year, 1753, Major George Washington was sent by Virginia's governor Robert Dinwiddie to Fort Le Boeuf, a French outpost in the Ohio River Valley. For the past sixty years, the British and French had been vying for control of the region. Washington's assignment was to deliver a message from Governor Dinwiddie, demanding that the French withdraw from British territory.

Washington led a small group of men on a difficult and dangerous journey across five hundred miles of wilderness. When he delivered Dinwiddie's demand, the

French commander rejected it, demanding instead that all English leave the area. Then he ordered that, from now on, the English would be arrested for trespassing. Washington noticed that the French were forming alliances with the local American Indian tribes. He returned to Williamsburg and informed Dinwiddie that the French intended to push their way into the Ohio River Valley.

In 1752, Washington inherited the twenty-five hundred-acre Mount Vernon plantation. He had little time to devote to managing the plantation that year. Governor Dinwiddie was determined to push the French back. He ordered Washington, now a lieutenant colonel, to lead an expedition against the French. Washington once again crossed the five hundred miles of wilderness, this time leading a four-hundred-man army.

When he reached the Ohio Valley, Washington led his men in a surprise attack on a camp of Frenchmen, killing ten of the enemy. That was the first battle in what came to be called the French and Indian War. Washington wrote in his diary, "I heard the bullets whistle, and believe me, there is something charming in the sound."[1]

The victory, however, was short-lived. The French were outraged. They claimed that Washington had attacked diplomats on their way to negotiate with the British. Expecting an attack by French troops from nearby Fort Duquesne, located at the site of present-day Pittsburgh, Pennsylvania, Washington had his men build a fort. Washington called the hastily built structure Fort Necessity. Two weeks later, a combined force of French soldiers and American Indians attacked Fort Necessity. The American Indians trusted neither the French nor the British, but they wanted to be allied with the winning side. They believed the French would prevail.

Washington suffered a total defeat at Fort Necessity. About one third of his men were killed, forcing him to sign papers of surrender. When he returned to Virginia, he resigned his commission with the Virginia militia. Apparently, when it came to the military, his enthusiasm was gone.

The next year, in June 1755, British general Edward Braddock arrived in Virginia with an army of fifteen hundred troops known as redcoats. His mission was to capture Fort Duquesne. When he asked Washington to accompany his army as a scout, Washington could not refuse.

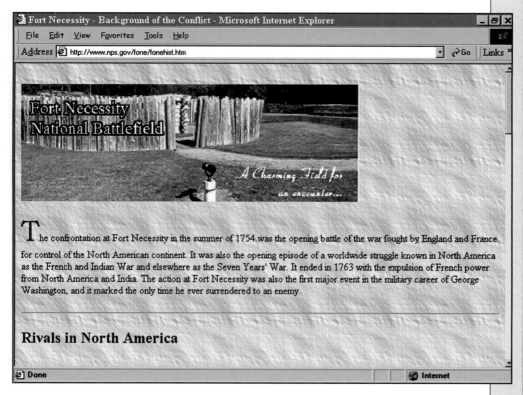

Fort Necessity - Background of the Conflict - Microsoft Internet Explorer

File   Edit   View   Favorites   Tools   Help

Address 🔁 http://www.nps.gov/fone/fonehist.htm   ▾ 𝒫 Go   Links »

Fort Necessity National Battlefield

A Charming Field for an encounter...

The confrontation at Fort Necessity in the summer of 1754 was the opening battle of the war fought by England and France for control of the North American continent. It was also the opening episode of a worldwide struggle known in North America as the French and Indian War and elsewhere as the Seven Years' War. It ended in 1763 with the expulsion of French power from North America and India. The action at Fort Necessity was also the first major event in the military career of George Washington, and it marked the only time he ever surrendered to an enemy.

Rivals in North America

🔁 Done   🌐 Internet

△ *After one early battle in the French and Indian War, Washington was forced to build a fort in the Ohio River Valley. He called it Fort Necessity. Soon after its construction, Washington was totally defeated at the fort by the French.*

▶ The Fighting Continues

General Braddock and his troops were trained in the traditional British fighting style. The men marched in orderly columns and rows. They expected their enemies to march straight up to them in the same orderly rows. The two armies were then supposed to fire away at each other until one side surrendered. Washington knew that the French troops and the American Indians did not fight in the same fashion. He tried, unsuccessfully, to persuade Braddock to change his tactics. Sure enough, on July 9, the French and their Indian allies carried out a surprise attack, firing from behind trees in the thick woods. Braddock was killed, as were about three hundred

▲ *After his service in the French and Indian War, George Washington returned home to Mount Vernon. In 1759 he married a wealthy widow named Martha Custis.*

redcoats. Washington led the surviving troops out of danger and back to Virginia.

In 1756, Britain and France formally declared war against each other, in what in Europe became known as the Seven Years War. Meanwhile, the French and Indian War in the colonies continued for several more years. Lieutenant Colonel George Washington once again commanded the Virginia troops. He led several expeditions against the French in the Ohio Valley. In 1759, the French abandoned their main fort in that area and lost some major battles. The war wound down as the British gained control of all disputed territories. The conflict officially ended in 1763.

By the end of 1758, Washington had returned home to Mount Vernon. He had tired of war and looked forward to peaceful years of farming. On January 6, 1759, he married Martha Custis, a wealthy widow. They managed the plantation. Washington became stepfather to Patsy and Jackie Custis. Now it was time for him to enjoy the life of a gentleman farmer.

Chapter 3 ▶

Hero of the American Revolution, 1759–1783

While the Washingtons were leading a quiet, peaceful life at home, events beyond Mount Vernon threatened to interfere with their happiness. After Britain and France signed a peace treaty in 1763, Parliament (Britain's law-making body) needed to find ways of paying for the expenses of the war. According to King George III and Parliament, the colonists should be taxed to share the cost of defending the empire.

▶ The Stamp Act

Until this time, the colonists paid only those taxes that they themselves had approved by a vote. The tax money raised was used to benefit each colony, not Britain. In 1765, the British Parliament passed the Stamp Act. The colonists would now be forced to pay a tax on many goods imported from England. The colonists felt this was unfair, and reacted with anger.

That year, Washington was elected to represent Fairfax County in the Virginia Assembly in Williamsburg. Its members were called burgesses. Patrick Henry and others spoke out against the Stamp Act, claiming that only the Virginia Assembly had the right to tax Virginians. Colonists of like mind spoke out in other American colonies. In response to colonial opposition, Britain repealed the Stamp Act.

In 1767, Parliament was still determined to raise taxes. Britain passed the Townshend Acts, which levied taxes on various imported goods, such as glass, lead, paint, paper, and tea. To Washington and others, it seemed as though Britain was trying to deprive the colonists of their rights as Englishmen.

Since the Stamp Act crisis in 1765, Washington had observed the growing rift between Britain and the colonies. He quietly began changing his way of life. Washington stopped importing products from England that Mount Vernon could do without. He also stopped growing tobacco, which he had previously grown mainly for export to England.

On April 5, 1767, Washington sent a letter to his neighbor and close friend George Mason, expressing his concern with the growing anticolonial British policies. He wrote, "At a time when our lordly Masters in Great Britain will be satisfied with nothing less than the deprivation of American freedom, it seems highly necessary that some-thing should be done to avert the stroke and maintain the liberty which we have derived from our ancestors."[1] In the letter, Washington called for a continent-wide boycott of British goods. He warned that if the boycott failed, Americans must be prepared to take up arms against the British government to protect their civil rights.

The Tea Tax

Relations between Britain and the colonies grew more tense and troubled over the next few years. In 1773, Boston merchants became enraged at the British East India Company's plan to sell tea at prices lower than American teas. This would ruin American businesses. On December 16, Boston merchants and their political allies crept aboard

East India Company ships. They dumped 342 chests of tea into the water. This American protest became known as the Boston Tea Party. Britain responded by passing the Intolerable Acts. In the spring of 1774, Britain closed off Boston Harbor to all ships and stationed a large number of troops in the city.

When the Virginia Assembly protested the British reactions, the royal governor dissolved the group. The burgesses continued to hold meetings in private. In September 1774, Washington and several other Virginia

▲ Angered by British plans to destroy the American tea business, the colonists revolted in 1773. They dumped 342 chests of tea into Boston Harbor. This act became known as the Boston Tea Party.

burgesses, among them Patrick Henry and George Mason, were elected to attend the First Continental Congress in Philadelphia. Delegates from all the other colonies except Georgia were gathered there.

There was general agreement that something must be done about the British. The delegates drew up a petition to send to King George, asserting the colonists' rights. Patrick Henry gave a rousing speech, declaring that the time had come to fight. He concluded with these words, "I know not what course others may take; but as for me, give me liberty or give me death!"[2] Another Congress was scheduled for the following year, to receive King George's answer to the petition.

In each colony, there were some people who remained loyal to King George and Parliament. They were known as loyalists or Tories. Those opposed to the British government were known as Patriots. In Massachusetts, Patriots called for an army of Minutemen who would be ready to march at a moment's notice.

Lexington and Concord

King George responded to the delegates' petition by sending more troops to the colonies. On April 19, 1775, in Lexington, Massachusetts, British troops and a group of Minutemen clashed, leaving eight Americans dead. No one knows who fired first, but the gunshot at the start of the battle came to be known as the "shot heard round the world." For years, the story of that battle inspired other people wishing to overthrow oppressive governments.

In May 1775, Washington attended the Second Continental Congress in Philadelphia as one of the delegates from Virginia. On June 15, upon the motion of John Adams, the delegates chose Washington to be commander

in chief of the Continental Army. Washington reluctantly accepted the responsibility. In a letter to Martha he wrote, "I assure you in the most solemn manner that so far from seeking this appointment, I have used every endeavor in my power to avoid it; not only from unwillingness to part from you and the family but from a consciousness of its being a trust too great for my capacity."[3] Washington would not see Mount Vernon again for six years.

▶ Commanding the Continental Army

Washington rode to Boston at the head of a small military force. There he took command of the main body of the fourteen-thousand-man Continental Army on July 3, 1775. The troops were untrained and undisciplined, but their bravery was unquestioned. On June 17, a force of fifteen hundred Patriots had fought against three thousand well-trained redcoats at Bunker Hill. By the time the Americans retreated, the British had lost more than a thousand men. Washington spent the rest of 1775 and early 1776 training his soldiers. Then, in March 1776, Washington's troops drove the British Army out of Boston.

The Second Continental Congress chose Washington as the commander in chief of the Continental Army. Although he did not want the position, he accepted, and led the army to victory over the British.

Washington correctly guessed that the British would soon try to take New York City. As a result, he moved his army south and prepared to defend it. Washington now had about seventeen thousand soldiers at his command. About one third of them were on Long Island, under the command of General Israel Putnam. The Patriots were outnumbered by the thirty thousand British troops and their Hessian hired guns.

Meanwhile, in June 1776, the Continental Congress met to decide whether the colonies should separate from Britain. Thomas Jefferson agreed to write a Declaration of Independence, which was adopted by the Congress on July 4. When Washington received a copy a few days later, he read it to his troops. The men listened in silence as their commander read, "When in the course of human events, it becomes necessary for one people to dissolve the political bands which have connected them with another. . . ." By the time he finished, cheers were sweeping through the ranks.

Unfortunately, for a time, revolutionary spirit proved to be no match for Britain's overwhelming military superiority. The Patriots lost one battle after another, beginning with the total defeat of Putnam's army on Long Island. Washington's forces were badly beaten in Brooklyn and Manhattan. With the remainder of his troops, Washington retreated to White Plains, New York, crossed the Hudson River to New Jersey, and made his way south to Pennsylvania.

▶ A Daring Attack

By December 1776, Washington and his troops were running out of strength and resources. Some members of Congress considered replacing Washington as commander

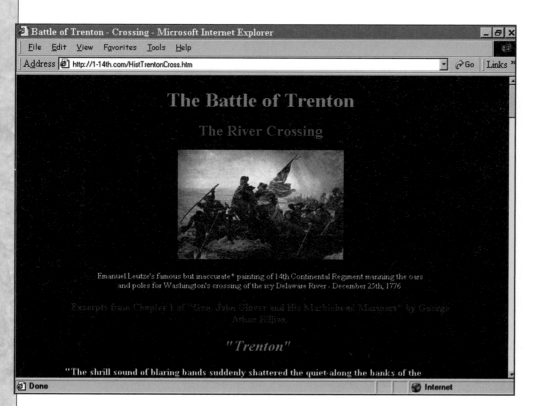

Battle of Trenton - Crossing - Microsoft Internet Explorer

File   Edit   View   Favorites   Tools   Help

Address   http://1-14th.com/HistTrentonCross.htm   Go   Links

The Battle of Trenton

The River Crossing

Emanuel Leutze's famous but inaccurate* painting of 14th Continental Regiment manning the oars
and poles for Washington's crossing of the icy Delaware River - December 25th, 1776.

Excerpts from Chapter 1 of "Gen. John Glover and His Marblehead Mariners" by George
Athan Billias.

"Trenton"

"The shrill sound of blaring bands suddenly shattered the quiet along the banks of the

Done   Internet

▲ *This famous painting by Emanuel Gottlieb Leutze gives an artist's impression of Washington's historic crossing of the Delaware River on December 25, 1776.*

in chief. Bold action was needed. On Christmas Day, during a howling snowstorm, a desperate Washington led his army across the Delaware River to gain a much-needed tactical advantage over the British. The next morning, Washington led the Americans in a successful surprise attack against the Hessians in Trenton. That bold gamble saved the faltering American Revolution.

Another bold maneuver followed a week later, on January 3, 1777, when Washington's troops defeated British general Charles Cornwallis's redcoats at Princeton,

New Jersey. The Americans then retreated before the British could regroup and retaliate.

Later that year, Washington and his eleven thousand troops attempted to defend Philadelphia. British general William Howe's fifteen thousand redcoats defeated the Americans at Brandywine Creek near Chad's Ford on September 11. On September 26, General Howe's forces entered Philadelphia. The Congress fled Philadelphia and set up headquarters in York, Pennsylvania.

Washington's army fought another battle with the British at Germantown, Pennsylvania, on October 4, and once again was defeated. Washington and his men retreated to nearby Valley Forge, where they could keep an eye on Howe's forces in Philadelphia.

On October 17, 1777, American general Horatio Gates's forces won a major victory over British general John Burgoyne's redcoats, at Saratoga, in what is now upstate New York. This marked a major turning point in the war. As a result, France, Britain's old enemy, agreed to an alliance with the American colonists. The French king, Louis XVI, recognized the independence of the colonies and sent military and economic aid, which was sorely needed. Meanwhile, the American troops spent a brutally cold winter at Valley Forge, where they suffered from shortages of food, clothing, and medical supplies.

Battle of Yorktown

In June 1778, British forces on their way from Philadelphia to New York were defeated by the Patriots in a battle at Monmouth, New Jersey. The war now shifted to the colonies in the South. Troops from both armies were constantly on the move. Numerous battles were fought in the Carolinas, Georgia, and Virginia. Finally, in October

1781, Washington's troops were joined by French reinforcements led by the Marquis de Lafayette. The combined force attacked the British Army under General Cornwallis at Yorktown, Virginia. Cornwallis and his eight thousand troops were surrounded by fourteen thousand French and American troops. On October 19, Cornwallis surrendered.

The war was over, for all practical purposes. The colonies had won their independence. The war officially

▲ Life as a Continental soldier was not easy. Many times the patriots did not have enough food, clothing, medical supplies, or shelter. Winters, like the one spent in Valley Forge, Pennsylvania, were especially harsh.

France Allied with American Colonies - Microsoft Internet Explorer

File   Edit   View   Favorites   Tools   Help

Address http://www.americaslibrary.com/pages/jb_0206_francoam_2_e.html   Go   Links »

Internet

▲ *Benjamin Franklin (shown here), John Jay, and John Adams negotiated the Treaty of Paris, ending the Revolutionary War.*

ended two years later, on September 3, 1783, with the signing of the Treaty of Paris.

In December 1783, Washington resigned as commander in chief of the Continental Army. He returned once again to his home, Mount Vernon, and to his beloved Martha. To Washington, nothing in the world seemed as appealing as resuming his life as a gentleman farmer.

Chapter 4 ▶ Private Citizen to President, 1783–1792

Washington returned home to Mount Vernon on December 24, 1783. Once again he enjoyed a private life. It was a great relief to have responsibilities no greater than managing of his own plantation. For the next four years, Washington was deeply involved in farm projects. He and Martha entertained guests at Mount Vernon, just as in the days before the war.

America was now independent, but the thirteen states were not yet unified. In 1781, while the war still raged,

▲ After the end of the Revolutionary War, Washington returned to Mount Vernon. This artist's account gives an overly generous impression of life there.

the Continental Congress had adopted the Articles of Confederation. The Articles provided for a central government, yet the central government had very limited powers.

▶ Shays' Rebellion

The need for a strong central government became clear in 1786. In Massachusetts that year, Daniel Shays organized an armed rebellion of farmers in protest against new taxes, this time levied by Massachusetts, not Britain. The rebellion was crushed on January 25, 1787, by a force of a thousand militiamen under the command of General William Shepherd. Still, Shays' Rebellion had alarmed many Americans, including George Washington. He realized that it had become urgent to create a strong central government.

A Constitutional Convention assembled in Philadelphia on May 25, 1787, for the purpose of drawing up a constitution setting forth the structure of the new government. The delegates, fifty-five at one time or another, chose Washington to preside over their meetings, which lasted until September 17. "The whole human race," said New York delegate Gouverneur Morris, "will be affected by the proceedings of this convention."[1]

The delegates debated various proposals for the new constitution over the next four months. James Madison of Virginia proposed a system of "checks and balances"—a separation of powers into the executive, legislative, and judicial branches. Power would also be divided between the federal and state governments, but with federal law taking precedence over state law.

▶ Elected President

The executive branch of government was to be headed by a president elected to a four-year term of office. The president would be chosen by electors from each state. On February 4, 1789, electors unanimously chose George Washington to be the first president of the United States. John Adams, who ran a distant second, became vice president.

Washington accepted his country's call to duty with great anxiety and trepidation. Indeed, at the time he told a friend, "My movements to the chair of government will be accompanied by feelings not unlike those of a culprit who is going to the place of execution."[2] He was very reluctant to give up his happy life at Mount Vernon, as was Martha.

▲ In February 1789, George Washington was unanimously elected to be the first president of the United States. This is an illustration of when he was sworn into office.

The tasks facing him as the nation's first president were truly daunting. Nation-building involved setting up a treasury, postal service, banks, and an army. Most important of all, Washington had to see to it that the states remained committed to building a strong, unified nation and did not go their separate ways.

On April 30, 1789, Washington took the oath of office at Federal Hall on New York City's Wall Street. Cheers rang out from the crowd who had come to witness the first inauguration of a United States president. Washington let it be known that he wanted to be addressed as "Mr. President," and not by any title suggestive of monarchy, such as "Your Excellency" or "Your Highness."

Martha Washington did not arrive in New York until the end of May. At first she was not very happy in New York and greatly missed Mount Vernon. In time, she and her husband would come to enjoy a busy social life that included balls, dances, and the theater.

The First Cabinet

To achieve his goal of a strong, unified nation, Washington chose the most qualified people to advise him. His cabinet consisted of Secretary of State Thomas Jefferson; Secretary of the

Martha Washington set the ► standard for future first ladies. Although she did not like New York at first, in time she grew to like her new home and busy social life.

Treasury Alexander Hamilton; Secretary of War Henry Knox; Attorney General Edmund Randolph; and Chief Justice John Jay of the Supreme Court.

Unfortunately, unity proved difficult to achieve in Washington's cabinet. Hamilton and Jefferson had very different visions of the nation they wished to create. Hamilton saw a nation of big cities and banks, industries and factories. Jefferson, on the other hand, wanted the nation to consist mainly of small farmers and craftsmen. These opposing views would lead to the formation of a two-party political system.

Washington tried to maintain a balance between Hamilton's Federalists and Jefferson's Democratic-Republicans. There were rarely easy solutions to their differences. When Hamilton proposed the creation of a Bank of the United States, Jefferson opposed the plan. To win Jefferson's support, Hamilton agreed to the creation of a national capital in a new Federal City, to be built on the Potomac River. The city became known as Washington, D.C. (the District of Columbia). In 1790, the nation's temporary capital was moved from New York City to Philadelphia, while the permanent capital was being built. Washington signed a bill in 1791 creating the first Bank of the United States, to be established in Philadelphia.

To keep his hand on the pulse of the nation, Washington traveled widely. In late 1789 he toured New England, and in 1791 he traveled throughout the southern states. Washington remained popular throughout his first term. In 1792 he was elected to a second term. John Adams was reelected vice president.

Chapter 5

Washington's Second Administration, 1793–1796

Washington was at the height of his popularity when his second presidential inauguration took place on March 4, 1793. As was the case in his first administration, Washington tried to balance the opposing points of view in his cabinet, but the rift grew even wider. Washington could not always remain impartial, and more and more he tended to side with Hamilton and the Federalists.

▶ Maintaining Neutrality

Damaging to Washington's reputation was his handling of foreign affairs. At first, Washington, Hamilton, and Jefferson were in agreement that foreign trade was vital to America's economic growth and well-being. They believed in the importance of maintaining friendly relations with the major powers, France and Britain. In 1793, though, France and Britain once again went to war with each other. Washington's problem was how to steer a neutral course between the two warring nations.

Washington would also have to figure out, if possible, a foreign policy that both Jefferson and Hamilton could live with. Unfortunately, this proved to be too difficult. Hamilton and the Federalists favored maintaining good relations with Britain, because of that country's economic strength. That policy was strongly opposed by Jefferson and the Democratic-Republicans. Jefferson had previously been

◀ *One of Washington's major challenges as president involved foreign affairs. He had to work closely with Thomas Jefferson (left) and Alexander Hamilton (below) to create a foreign policy that best suited the country's needs.*

the U.S. ambassador to France. He had supported the French Revolution in 1789, and still favored the French. Also, many Americans still felt grateful to France for that nation's support during the American Revolution, and they still mistrusted the British.

Making Washington's job even more difficult were Britain's actions on the high seas. The British Navy regularly seized American ships bound for France. The British were also forcing American sailors to serve on British warships. This practice was known as impressment. Washington issued a Proclamation of Neutrality in April 1793, but Britain ignored America's neutrality.

Washington then sent John Jay, Chief Justice of the U.S. Supreme Court, to Britain to negotiate a treaty. The following year saw the signing of the Jay Treaty of 1794. When terms of the treaty were made public in 1795, Jefferson and the Democratic-Republicans were outraged. They saw the treaty as caving in to British demands. After heated debate

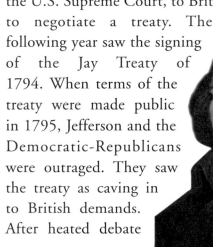

and angry protests, Congress ratified the Jay Treaty. Unfortunately, British interference with American shipping did not end.

While foreign policy occupied much of Washington's attention, domestic problems arose. Perhaps the most serious problem resulted from a tax on whiskey. Back in 1791, during Washington's first administration, Hamilton had proposed the whiskey tax, and Congress had passed it into law. Farmers in western Pennsylvania protested the tax because it prevented them from profiting from their surplus grain. The farmers had been producing rye whiskey from the grain and selling it throughout the region.

▶ Whiskey Rebellion

Over the next couple of years, the farmers organized a tax resistance movement and refused to pay the whiskey tax. In the summer of 1794, a force of two thousand armed farmers threatened to attack the federal garrison in Pittsburgh. Washington realized that the time had come to put an end to the Whiskey Rebellion. Washington and Hamilton rode toward Pittsburgh at the head of an army of thirteen thousand men. This show of force frightened the whiskey rebels. By the time Washington's army reached its destination, the rebels had scattered in all directions. The Whiskey Rebellion was over. Washington eventually pardoned the two rebel leaders who had been sentenced to prison.

On September 17, 1796, Washington gave his Farewell Address to the nation. The address was not given as a speech, but was published in the newspapers. In it, he warned Americans of the dangers of excessive political bickering between members of the newly-formed political parties. He stressed how important it was to strive for

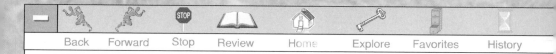
unity on major issues in order to build a strong nation. He cautioned the nation to avoid becoming entangled in permanent alliances with foreign nations.

Although his popularity had seriously declined during the past four years, many Americans wanted Washington to run for a third term. Washington declined, and some Americans were not sorry to see him go. Regardless of people's wishes at the time, Washington set an important precedent by refusing to serve more than two terms in office. This precedent was not broken until Franklin D. Roosevelt's third administration in the 1940s.

Chapter 6 ▶

Last Years at Mount Vernon, 1797–1799

George and Martha Washington were eager to return to the beautiful, quiet countryside of their Mount Vernon plantation. Washington was worn out from the political battles of the past four years. At President John Adams's inauguration in Philadelphia on March 4, 1797, Washington sat off to one side. Adams could not help but notice, with some dismay, that more eyes in the audience were on Washington than on him. Adams later wrote, "He seemed to enjoy a triumph over me. Methought I heard him say, 'Ay, I'm fairly out and you're fairly in. See which of us will be happiest!'"[1]

▶ Good to be Home

Indeed, Washington was happy to be heading home to Mount Vernon. Once there, just as in the old days, Washington took to managing his plantation with enthusiasm. Work needed to be done on buildings that had fallen into disrepair.

John Adams became the second president on March 4, 1797. Washington was asked to run for a third term, but he declined. Because of this action, it became customary for presidents to only serve two terms.

Washington was busy most of the time. When not galloping about his fields on horseback and tending to agricultural matters, he wrote a lot of letters. He and Martha once again enjoyed receiving guests, and there were many visitors.

In 1798, trouble was brewing between the United States and France. President Adams requested Washington's help in military preparations. On July 11, Washington reluctantly agreed to become commander in chief of the military again. Although he never saw active duty, he helped in planning the organization of a new national army. One of the tasks that he particularly enjoyed was helping to design the army's uniforms. Ever since his childhood fascination with his older half brother's British Army uniform, Washington had been interested in military uniforms. So he took this opportunity to design a blue coat with yellow buttons and silver stars.

▶ A Somber Moment

The following year, on a cold day in December, Washington came home complaining of a severe sore throat. He had been riding around Mount Vernon in freezing rain and sleet. Several days later, on December 14, 1799, the nation's first president, and one of its greatest leaders in peacetime as well as in war, died at the age of sixty-seven. Washington had presided over the creation of the new American nation. Under his wise leadership and that of the able men he chose for his cabinet, the residents of the thirteen states more and more began to see themselves as Americans instead of citizens of individual states.

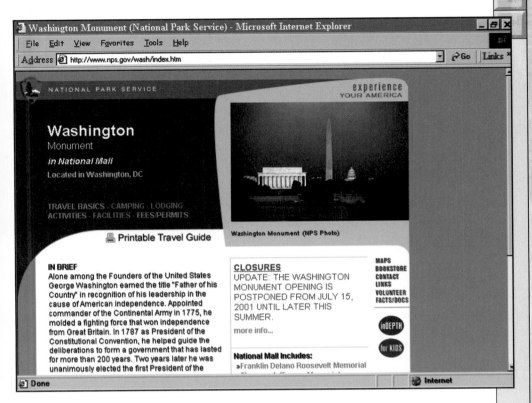

Washington Monument (National Park Service) - Microsoft Internet Explorer

File   Edit   View   Favorites   Tools   Help

Address   http://www.nps.gov/wash/index.htm   Go   Links

NATIONAL PARK SERVICE

experience YOUR AMERICA

Washington
Monument
in National Mall
Located in Washington, DC

TRAVEL BASICS · CAMPING · LODGING
ACTIVITIES · FACILITIES · FEES/PERMITS

🖨 **Printable Travel Guide**

Washington Monument (NPS Photo)

IN BRIEF
Alone among the Founders of the United States
George Washington earned the title "Father of his
Country" in recognition of his leadership in the
cause of American independence. Appointed
commander of the Continental Army in 1775, he
molded a fighting force that won independence
from Great Britain. In 1787 as President of the
Constitutional Convention, he helped guide the
deliberations to form a government that has lasted
for more than 200 years. Two years later he was
unanimously elected the first President of the

CLOSURES
UPDATE: THE WASHINGTON
MONUMENT OPENING IS
POSTPONED FROM JULY 15,
2001 UNTIL LATER THIS
SUMMER.

more info...

National Mall includes:
»Franklin Delano Roosevelt Memorial

MAPS
BOOKSTORE
CONTACT
LINKS
VOLUNTEER
FACTS/DOCS

inDEPTH
for KIDS

Done   🌐 Internet

▲ *Through his years of service, George Washington
helped America become a unified nation. The
Washington Monument pays tribute to one of
America's most important leaders.*

On December 26, General Henry "Light Horse
Harry" Lee, another hero of the Revolutionary
War, delivered the "Funeral Oration Upon George
Washington" before the Congress. He declared that
Washington was "first in war, first in peace, first in the
hearts of his countrymen."[2]

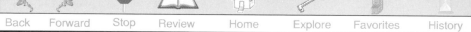
Chapter 1. A Bold Gamble, December 25, 1776

1. Thomas Paine, *The American Crisis*, excerpt, published December 19, 1776, quoted in Willard Sterne Randall, *George Washington: A Life* (New York: Henry Holt and Company, 1997), p. 323.

2. Willard Sterne Randall, *George Washington: A Life* (New York: Henry Holt and Company, 1997), p. 322.

Chapter 2. Early Years, 1732–1759

1. George Washington quoted in Carter Smith, ed., *The Founding Presidents* (Brookfield, Conn.: The Millbrook Press, 1993), p. 22.

Chapter 3. Hero of the American Revolution, 1759–1783

1. Willard Sterne Randall, *George Washington: A Life* (New York: Henry Holt and Company, 1997), p. 236.

2. Ibid., p. 273.

3. Ibid., pp. 284–285.

Chapter 4. Private Citizen to President, 1783–1792

1. Paul F. Boller, Jr., and Jean Tilford, *This Is Our Nation* (St. Louis: Webster Publishing Company, 1961), p. 147.

2. Willard Sterne Randall, *George Washington: A Life* (New York: Henry Holt and Company, 1997), p. 437.

Chapter 6. Last Years at Mount Vernon, 1797–1799

1. James Thomas Flexner, *Washington: The Indispensable Man* (Boston: Little, Brown and Company, 1969), p. 357.

2. Joseph Nathan Kane, *Facts About the Presidents* (New York: The H. W. Wilson Company, 1981), p. 16.

Further Reading

Ferrie, Richard. *The World Turned Upside Down: George Washington and the Battle of Yorktown.* New York: Holiday House, 1998.

Flexner, James Thomas. *George Washington: The Forge of Experience.* Boston: Little, Brown and Company, 1965.

———. *Washington: The Indispensable Man.* Boston: Little, Brown and Company, 1969.

Kane, Joseph Nathan. *Facts About the Presidents.* New York: The H. W. Wilson Company, 1981.

Old, Wendie, C. *George Washington.* Springfield, N.J.: Enslow Publishers, Inc., 1997.

Osborne, Mary Pope. *George Washington: Leader of a New Nation.* New York: Dial Books for Young Readers, 1991.

Randall, Willard Sterne. *George Washington: A Life.* New York: Henry Holt and Company, 1997.

Rosenberg, John M. *First in Peace: George Washington, the Constitution, & the Presidency.* Brookfield, Conn.: Millbrook Press, 1998.

Welsbacher, Anne. *George Washington.* Minneapolis, Minn.: ABDO Publishing Company, 1998.